MW00768575

Kendra
Benford

God
Bless!

My Heart

Poems of Love

My Heart

Poems of Love

Kendra "Niki" Benford

Printed in the United States of America

First Printing, 2017

Editor: Ashley Davis
Cover Design: Ministering Moments Photography
Interior Design/Layout: Iris M Williams

ISBN-13: 978-1-942022-91-6
ISBN10: 1942022913

Iris M Williams

The Butterfly Typeface Publishing
PO BOX 56193
Little Rock Arkansas 72215

Dedication

To my grandfather and mother.

"If you don't believe in yourself, no one else will. God gives his toughest battles to his strongest soldiers. Don't give up yet, God always has you regardless!"

-Kendra "Niki" Benford

Table of Contents

Foreword

My grandfather and I would often have conversations over the phone about me "...using my gift before I lose it." I explained to him that I just wrote for fun and to express myself when I feel like no one listens to me.

Grandfather continued to preach about why I should do write.

Unfortunately, when I finally gave consideration to what he was saying, he passed away from cancer.

Like grandfather, my mother urged me to write as well. My mother also passed away and she too will not see my talent grow into what she and grandfather knew in their heart it would be.

Mother gives me the motivation to keep moving forward.

Acknowledgment

I would like to thank my family and friends who continually help me strive for greatness.

A special thanks to Ms. Iris Williams for believing in me and giving my poetry a chance to inspire others.

Introduction

I started writing poetry and short stories when I was thirteen. A childhood friend was the first one to point out my talent. That was how we bonded; we shared an interest in writing.

For me writing has always been fun, even before I knew I loved it. I used to write short stories for the writing portion in elementary school. This was when EOC's (End of course) were called EOG's (End of grade testing.)

Besides music, my only passion was writing. I just always loved to write. Like music, writing helped me escape life, express myself emotionally, and inspire or explain the way I see myself or today's world.

My hope for my writing is to inspire others, continue making my family proud and to make my mother smile.

Kendra "Niki" Benford

Don't forget yourself

and put everything else at stake

remember you still have

a valuable heart rate.

Kendra "Niki" Benford

Special Little lady

I've been through trials of hell and many
different bad trans-creations.
Sometimes I wonder to myself, "Have I
really learned my lesson?"

Yet even when I don't deserve it, my God
keeps sending me blessings.
No relationship needed.

My heart needs time,
so my emotions can feed it.
Giving your all to someone just to end up
being dropped,
it really makes you wonder, "What's the
other person got?"

Then you have to take account for
yourself and make the cycle stop.

Love begins being hidden
when there is no story being written.

Kendra "Niki" Benford

Sex is at its best
when there is no heart being put to the
test.
People want easy not hard.
Why does love consistently drift away
and starve?

Baby after baby,
but there is no one to speak.

Marry me first
because the relationship ends
with a constant procedure of broken
trust.

That's why love, to me, has become
a fragment of useless dust.

I can change somebody's life.
I can even be a faithful wife,
but looking at where I came from,
all that just doesn't feel right.
A baby to hold is what made me pray on a
maybe,
but my God told me it all happens in time

My special little lady.

Kendra "Niki" Benford

Heart Rate

Hate, now that's something very strong,
but in this case, it shouldn't matter for the
awful road I've been on.

I've been looking for love for so long,
I forgot to think about how I am in control
of my own song.

Love is hidden a lot
Because, nowadays, sex is all we got.
To me, I still think there is more to life,
and someone out there is faithful enough
to make me his wife.

I'm not going to lie;
I gave up a time or two,
but that was all because of you.

Trial and error is what I was often told.
Therefore, with that being said,
my heart can't be sold.

Kendra "Niki" Benford

Weed out the snakes
so God can show you what's fate.
Don't forget yourself,
and put everything else at stake.
Remember, you still have
a valuable heart rate.

Pretty Precious SNAKE

Hello pretty, pretty precious SNAKE,
would you mind if I play with you
like children play with cake?

Well sure,
if you're ready for me to take away
every opportunity you had to make?
I'm confused;
why would you do that to me?

You seem just as friendly as can be.
What do you mean,
I'm a snake for goodness sake...
I slither around just to see
what I can take.

Well I've been playing with you for a
while, and you haven't bitten me yet.
That's because I haven't placed my bet
to make a good enough set.

Kendra "Niki" Benford

I don't get it; why are you being so mean?
Oh, my skin hasn't shed enough
for it to be fully seen.

OUCH! Why did you bite me?
Had enough? Don't you see,
just how strong my venom is
if you choose to keep me.

Why do you keep biting me?

I love you, and I'm just trying
to be a friend and figure out
the next best thing to do.

OUCH! Ah! Bite number two
and I see you put me down now.

I guess I'm not as friendly
when no one else is around.
Why won't you let me play with you?

Because my heart is no good for you,
even my own family
couldn't help me through.

Kendra "Niki" Benford

Had enough of playing tough?

Why are you no good for me to keep?

Because I carry a lot of secrets,
I have to make sure no one says a peep
or else I won't get good sleep.

Why would you bare secrets?

To keep away suspicion just in case
someone gets smart to listen.

I still love you just the same.

Why can't you show me the way?

Because I was NEVER supposed to stay.

Honey, there are others like me....
OUCH! Ah!

I caught you off guard.
Who else do you know who wouldn't love
to take charge?

Kendra "Niki" Benford

What do you mean by that?

Be careful with friends even loved ones
past and future... why?

Because if you don't get wise,
people seen and unseen
will shatter your heart like a bat.

Just remember I told you that.

Kendra "Niki" Benford

You need to be wise and listen to reason,
but God, I am just so tired of my heart
repeatedly bleeding,
when all I want to do is begin the leading.

With healing takes time.

Trust Me; you will have your moment to
shine.

It's the constant mistakes I make
that make me question
how much suffering can I take.

I think about it so much
I literally can feel my heart ache
with each step, I continue to take.

You want to know why? Why?

Because you're getting closer to me and
what's to be even if people try
to bring you down with repetitive lies.

Kendra "Niki" Benford

Maybe it's a sign
that they shouldn't be around
because all they're doing right now
is continuing to let you drown.

Hold on to your faith to get your blessing,
because with every suffering
out comes a lesson.

Walking Contradictions

Walking contradictions,
what are they to you?

I say it just depends on what people do.
Be careful whom you meet,
if you're not sure
on what they intend to seek.

You've got to walk the way you talk;
your actions show your heart,
so be aware of what you start.

Lies don't heal; they just make it
a little easier for people to deal.

When they can't handle something real,
people portray a specific image.

It doesn't mean that they really feel it.

Walking contradictions are like snakes;
their true intention is to be fake.

Kendra "Niki" Benford

So be careful what you take in
because they can be purifying your heart
with sin.

Marriages and relationships are a joke
to some,
looking at how people act within them
now makes me want to go numb.

I don't claim to walk with GOD
or act like I sit on a thrown next to Jesus,
but I do believe in His embracing power.

There is a happily ever after.

Watch what you do and say
because you will have to answer to Him
one day.

Kendra "Niki" Benford

Be Careful

If you give something to God,
that's for Him to keep and to fix.

You can't give it to God
and still keep holding onto it.

That just shows them
that you're not quite over it.

But you tell yourself,
"Hey it will eventually go away."

Sadly, that's not the case.

Then, your mind begins to wonder,
"Why give your heart to someone
who's constantly slapping you
in the face?"

Your heart doesn't know much anymore.

That's why it is slowly
stepping toward the door.

Kendra "Niki" Benford

I vow to stop the damage
that I can no longer manage.

The heart is rare and easy to shatter
so be careful
when you say "someone matters."

Be free to love hard
and live life to its fullest,
but also remember God never needs His
child to be foolish.

Share your burdens; share your cares
with the man that always sits upstairs.
Behind every want, there is also a more
powerful need.

Be careful how you make your choices
when you're saying what you mean
because I thought love meant one team.

Kendra "Niki" Benford

Watch

This little girl with such immature
thoughts and insecure vibes,
that thought alone
nearly made her lose her mind.

Family wars, and broken hearts,
she thought her life had ended
before she even got a fresh start.

Constantly fighting
between who's right and who's wrong
will make you wonder,
"Was she ever that strong?"

Healing battle wounds
to reach some kind of common ground,
makes her wonder
if anyone cares enough
to keep her around?

She's trying not to drown
from her deepest fear,
trying to hold on to her last tear.

Kendra "Niki" Benford

Love is meant to keep,
but words can cut deep.

Watch what you say and what you do,
because you wouldn't like it
if someone did it to you.

That's the thing
that brings insecurities to the table.

The thing that makes girls unable
because they feel like they're held
under an unwritten label,
which makes them believe
love is an untrue fable.

Love that little girl enough
to make things right,
that way she can enjoy life
to become somebody's wife.

Don't always do things out of spite.

Kendra "Niki" Benford

Old School Love

Is it us, or just you?

Because at one point in time
I thought we meant two.

Two people chasing dreams.

Two people becoming one team,
that's what love is to me.

That old school love exists no more,
where true Romeos spread roses
on the floor
and are not afraid to open every door.

Nope, never, that love left here
because of constant bad weather.

Guys look at pretty face and nice hips.

They just don't know some of those girls
will be the first to dip.

Kendra "Niki" Benford

Disrespect is not what makes you
attractive,
faithfulness and good love
now that's what gets you satisfied action.

Actions always speak louder than words.

Without that, you're just broken glass
that fell in love way to fast
that held onto something
that was never meant to last.

My heart has a key,
but my mind has a say too.

Don't let everybody get that close to you.

When it's real, my GOD will heal
until then I'll just sit back and deal.

Kendra "Niki" Benford

The Chase

To the girl growing up
that never felt protection from others
and has never felt secure within herself
growing up feeling insecure
and distant from everybody else.

When she looks into the mirror
all she sees are flaws
build up from years of broken walls.

Beautiful, intelligent,
why do you make life seem so irrelevant?

Girls on social networks
showing every ounce of skin,
when your body is supposed to be
your secret temple from within.

We, as women, need to be aware
of the attention that we attract,
because whatever is given away or said
cannot be taken back.

Kendra "Niki" Benford

Ladies, don't be with someone
out of the fear of being alone
because love can be like
an unwritten song.

To the men who pursue women
with an open mind but a closed heart,
you shouldn't have approached her from
the start.

Love yourself and GOD will let everything
fall into its rightful place,
because everything that circles around
you is not worth the chase.

Kendra "Niki" Benford

Inspiration

"You are an inspiration to me,"
what does that tell you?

Well I have a few answers for the heart
that doesn't have a clue.

That means giving someone hope
when they'd scream,
"GOD, I THINK I'M AT THE END
OF MY ROPE!"

With me not doing anything,
I gained back everything.

When people see me,
they see that faith is real,
and with prayer
there isn't anything GOD can't heal.

Used, disrespected, loved, abandoned
and almost met eye to eye with death,
I still rose above with a smile and said

Kendra "Niki" Benford

"Okay Devil, what do you have for me
next?"

Because I know,
my GOD isn't finished with me yet.

He always has my back
even when I fall a little off track.

I am an inspiration to all
even when I am out there doing wrong,
my GOD keeps me strong to never fall.

So, when people say,
"You are an inspiration to me,"
it shows me that I have a purpose in life,
and I wouldn't make too bad of a wife.

Until that day comes for me,
I'll keep my fight to know what's right.

Heart of gold, mind of intelligence,
why would I listen to anything else
that's irrelevant?

Don't settle for less;
go for something greater.

Kendra "Niki" Benford

You don't want to end up regretting years
later.

"You are an inspiration to me."

I know that this statement is true,
but what will this mean
if someone says it to you?

Relationships

Toleration plus frustration equals
deterioration.

Is your life worthy to you,
or do you enjoy being black and blue?

Look into the eyes of your children;
they see what you do.

Always remember
they're a little reflection of you.

Close your eyes, and shut your ears
only to be blinded and to be afraid
of the things you might hear.

What happened to common courtesy
and talking things through
instead of people always wanting
to put their hands on you.

Kendra "Niki" Benford

Don't stay where there's no room for you
to be kept,
because you were always taught
to do your best.

In life, you have choices
no matter how tough the situation is,
with or without kids.

Some problems are different however.
Some people just face a lot of bad
weather.

You always have that person saying,"
Don't worry it'll get better,
because we can make it through
anything together."

You try and you fight
just to get one situation right,
but what if in the end
you hold on too tight?

Then lose everyone else in sight.

Kendra "Niki" Benford

Relationships can go either way,
but it's the things you do and say
to make that person decide
if they want to stay or to walk away.
Right or wrong, just stay strong.

Be careful of the drama you bring upon
yourself,
because it might just hurt somebody else.

Speak your mind and just get whatever it
is you have to say out;
don't let your mind wonder
as you sit in silence and pout.

Be wise of your words that you fear
because words hurt
if you hadn't noticed my dear.

Love hard and be true;
don't let anything or anyone change you!

Kendra "Niki" Benford

Fate

There once was a little girl
who had inspirational dreams.

She was trying to figure out
everything the world means.

With a heart so big made out of gold,
she would always turn her cheek
to the negativity that was told.

She knew her love
was too good to be sold.

A little smile and a dose of GOD
are the only things she needed,
because she knew with that
there was no way she could be defeated.

"Stand tall and be proud of who you are,"
is what she always said.

No one accomplishes anything
sitting around in bed.

Kendra "Niki" Benford

Live life not regret,
because your success isn't finished yet.

Go through the storm,
but don't let it abuse you
because you don't know
when GOD is ready to use you.

She didn't know
how empowering she could be,
until that little girl grew up to be me.

"How do I know this," you may ask.

Well, it's all in the mindset
if you're capable to finish the task.

Yes, it is a hard race to run,
but I always believed
in getting the job done.

I've been hurt in many ways
that you wouldn't even believe.

Countless, exhausting times of being
deceived, but that only made me stronger
in hopes to achieve.

Kendra "Niki" Benford

When a person shows you who they are,
the truth is not that far.

The devil was once an angel too,
so be careful of the people you choose.

I'm climbing for my destiny,
regardless of how many rocks
are thrown at me.

I work for GOD not you,
so what else do you plan to do?

2014 is coming sooner than you know,
so are you going to take this year
to finally grow?

Don't wait,
too late to change the obstacle of fate
because you'll mess around
and miss your due date.

Kendra "Niki" Benford

Angelic Feathers

To get into something new
you have to follow to what's true.

Do you want to be tagged to a king
or to follow someone else's dream?

It's all who you allow to be on your team.
My father said, "Never let a man treat you
like less than the queen you are.
Remember that God
has taken you way too far."

Beautiful young woman
with true intentions,
so they won't feel anything is missing.

They need to come together
and build each other up
not manipulate one another
with misguided mistrust.

Kendra "Niki" Benford

Instead of arguing constantly between
each other
and be forgotten in minutes
like a little fragment of dust.

We matter to do better,
remember we are one of God's angel's
angelic feathers.

We are raised to be intelligently clever
in God's everlasting favor.

For some women
it's hard to come together
and take on this cruel world forever.

So many are being snakes
flashing hard to be fake
trying to fight against each other
to win an unwinnable race
instead of waiting
on a little thing called fate.

So God told me to tell you all
to slow up your pace.

Kendra "Niki" Benford

Going Down

Vulnerability is a *itch,
especially when you have a constant itch.

Paranoid and afraid to hurt the familiar,
constantly worried
about what others will think,
wanting to try the unfamiliar
but worried about if my heart will sink.

Sometimes I wonder,
will the worry ever fade,
or maybe this is how I was made.

I really shouldn't care about anything
or anyone,
but as the saying goes,
everyone needs someone.

When everyone has claimed you
for the good girl type,
you try constantly to do everything right.

Kendra "Niki" Benford

That way you'll get to sleep peacefully
at night.

But there are these new experiences
that are in my way,
that grab at me and beg me
to come out and play.

Stick with the old or go with the new.
My body's so torn
that I don't know what to do.

The truth can come and go just like that,
but do I have the faith
to believe it's coming back?

I'm happy by doing me;
isn't this the way life is supposed to be?

I want to be used by you
if it's what you ask of me,
but what if I can't handle it
after I become a we?

Trust in me you say,
but what if my heart doesn't want
it to go down that way?

Kendra "Niki" Benford

My Heart

A heart takes on everything
the mind cannot accept,
but is it wrong
that the heart urges payback?

Love, honesty, and respect
are all that were asked,
but if you're not true to yourself,
that's a tough task.

So what choices do you have
if you had one object to save?

Your heart or your intelligent brain,
which one is easier to tame
after you're over being ashamed?

How do you go
from the inside looking out
to the outside looking in,
when the answer is obvious,
but it's up to you to kick it in.

Kendra "Niki" Benford

Some people and decisions
are given to you as life's blessings,
but be aware of the things you say
and of the company you keep
because talk is always cheap.

If you are willing to make someone
your king or queen,
why let someone stay in between?

That decision is only up to you,
whether you want to go solo
or follow through with something new.

You can't raise the grown;
they already know the definition
to holding their own.

That doesn't mean you have to play
the same song.

People change with time
just as easy as I
can come up with a rhyme,

Kendra "Niki" Benford

but be cautious
because an old dog can
always learn new tricks,
so always pack your heart with bricks.

Guarded

The pain that's within,
take it away so my heart can mend.

Trust where and trust who, "Oh no,"
my trust was gone the minute I lost you.

My heart is guarded and doesn't want
to let go just so it can be bombarded.

Save me; I beg.

Revive me although I fear
my heart is already dead.

Save me; take away
what's already been said.

Walk around being love's joke.

I'm surprised I didn't begin to choke
on every lie spoke.

Kendra "Niki" Benford

Save me; remind me
what's the definition of family?

Save me, for I am on my knees.

I don't want my heart
to continue to bleed.

I try to guard it and even try to freeze it.

Find a secret place
somewhere and leave it.

Save me to close the door
where my heart was left
shattered on the floor.

I'm lost; I'm stuck
and unfortunately walk around
holding a heart with no trust.

Happy is what shows
but if only outsiders knew
how many low blows people threw.

Save me cause I'm running
out of things to do.

Kendra "Niki" Benford

Being held is what I feel I need,
but I keep telling others to leave.

I'm honestly not this mean.

Save me to change me and to show me
how love is supposed to be.

I use to say there is no me without you;
now all I wish for is my grandma
to still be here.

She will indeed tell me what to do,
but if no one is in sight,
I wonder if anything is worth the fight.

That says a lot for some
that have lost faith twice.

I just have to take my chance
and roll the dice.

Kendra "Niki" Benford

Wish I Could Talk to You

I wish I could talk to you
because besides a child,
your love I felt was true.

My heart, you never fought it;
our bond was grand
before I knew it even started.

I wish I could talk to you
because you are the only one
in this moment
who can tell me what to do.

Your face, I try my best not to forget
a trace,
and believe me
no one can take your place.

I wish I could talk to you
because I'm not going to lately.

I've been feeling a little blue
all because I've been lost without you.

Kendra "Niki" Benford

You always believe I can do anything.
And you tell me
to never let anyone make me feel bad
so why so often do I feel sad?

I wish I could talk to you
maybe then I'll stop constantly breaking
what's left of my heart
and finally believe, I can have a new start.

Missing you is an understatement,
because you can no longer ask me,
"What goals are you making?"

I'm happy to say your baby graduated.

I knew you were smiling down saying,
"You finally made it."

I love you, and yes, I wish you were here,
but I now understand
why you left with no fear
because God whispered and said,
"I now need you near..."

Kendra "Niki" Benford

Unborn

I feel you with me as if it was meant to be,
but God whispers that it is not time for us
to become a we.

When I go to sleep at night,
I can almost swear I hear your cries,
and every time I wake up,
a part of my heart dies.

Being denied the chance
to hold your little hands and feet
makes me sometimes want
to argue with God
as to when will it be our moment to meet.

All He says back is,
"Please my child,
have a little more faith in Me."

I see your beautiful face
in every child I look at.

Kendra "Niki" Benford

It makes me swear on the many years
I passed up whispering,
"I wish I can have them all back."

But let's face the fact
that we sadly do not have the power
to back track.

Honesty and family
that's all I ever wanted to have and to be,
but it's tiresome
because every time I look,
no one wants to take a shot
and to believe in me.

So my dreams of holding you one day
will have to wait for us to become a we
because tragically that happy ending
was taken from me.

So I wish well on others
who don't deserve it
because I know one day soon
it'll all be worth it.

Kendra "Niki" Benford

My faith is all I have left
and half a heart to possibly give
because I know at the very end
my God is going to allow me to win.

Wheelchair Swag

The reasons and lessons
that I learn everyday
don't always make the pain go away.

People say, with time, the heart will heal.

Meanwhile, I want to bandage
it up with something real.

People are more interested
in what's in between
or too busy asking the next girl
" A yo baby, why you gotta be so mean?"

Intelligence is what keeps women strong
And helps them know the difference
between right and wrong.

I'm a pretty girl
with too much wheelchair swag
that I carry it all in one makeup bag.

Kendra "Niki" Benford

Be who you are
and not who people tell you to be
because as you can see
I'm happy just being me.

If you don't like what I said,
there's the door.

I don't have time to keep cleaning up
other people's messes on the floor.

Get to know my mind if anything
because if not, you'll miss everything.

Flaws and all,
but I wear them and stand tall.

Never hate
because you'll miss out on your fate.

Forgive and forget,
but never be misled
because you'll overlook
what's already been said.

Kendra "Niki" Benford

When Doves Cry

Times changes a lot ...
Tragedies make you hold things in a box.

Concealed but never
spoken to be revealed.

Mommy, I have so much to tell,
but the only thing I can do now
is wish you well.

Some days it's hard for me to breathe,
and in certain situations,
you'd tell me to just get up and to leave.

I don't have that inner voice;
so sometimes I make myself feel
like I have no choice.

No heart, so I can't feel;
it's my unique way of learning to deal.

Kendra "Niki" Benford

Disrespect is constantly thrown my way,
but I act like it doesn't affect me
day to day.

"Give them your behind to kiss,"
is what you would say,
but I don't know how
and that's why I stay.

Death should leave growth and change,
at least it has for me in another range.

Dad is still here,
but I still dream with a broken heart
because I desperately desire a new start.

Walked over by an illusion of love
that sometimes I wish to fly away
like a lonely dove.

Like your favorite song
"When Doves Cry,"
it's hard not to, even when I try.

Staying silent is the best thing I can do
because there is no me without you.

Kendra "Niki" Benford

Future is a myth to me
because some things will just never be.

Past being renewed
so what is there left to do
because no one will ever love your Poo
the way you do.

All in all, Mommy, I will forever miss you...

Our Mess

Fast to love, but weary to forgive,
which one do you choose to live?

With living in this world of doubt,
I don't see how anyone
can figure anything out.

Bringing someone down
just to lift another up,
all that shows anyone
is that you haven't grown up.

We all have flaws
and we should own them with pride,
but we have others
that are ashamed to take that ride.

They'd much rather run and hide.

Trust is the main thing
that holds people together,
but what if they're always
getting tossed into bad weather?

Kendra "Niki" Benford

People always judge one another,
and manipulate more than twice
maybe one day will get things right.

Until then be happy and don't stress
because GOD will always fix our mess.

Kendra "Niki" Benford

Her Number One Girl

My mommy holds my hand
on my wedding day
and talks me through my own Labor Day.

If only God would've made it that way,
sadly, He whispered to her and said,
"My child I am sorry you cannot stay."

My future was bright,
and it felt like everything was going right.

Now it's a struggle to even sleep at night
because she is not there
to tell me everything will be alright.

She always dreamed
I'd be respected and loved
by the man of my dreams,
but she also told me to be humble and
never too mean.

Kendra "Niki" Benford

She dreamed I'd inspire the world,
even if I didn't,
I'd still be her number one girl.

Soulful

I've never had to fight,
but lately I don't know my left
from my right.

What makes it even harder to fight
is when the devil slips in
and beats up my soul at night.

I want to yell out
"I quit, I had enough
of this heart aching trip!"

But a tiny piece of strength tells me not to
because I might skip something
I never really wanted to miss.

Future, "Do I have you?"

To my past, "I want to destroy you."

To my present,
What am I supposed to do?

Kendra "Niki" Benford

What do I do
with a heart that feels invisible?
What do I do with a person who thinks
every action he or she does is admissible?

Right now, life is making me
purely miserable.

A heart of gold that no one can see,
people can't tell
that love is really killing me.

Quite often
the world I live in feels like Hell,
but I promised my mother,
I would not dwell.

When you try to get your life right,
that's when the devil holds on tight.

That's when everyone begins to lose sight
of their hopes and dreams
they wished for at night.

Don't let him win,
because God picks his strongest soldiers
from the bottom of the bin.

Kendra "Niki" Benford

One True Captain

Being encouraged is hard to do
when all through my mind
memories overflow of you.

Everyone tells me to ask God
and He will tell me what to do.

I fall to my knees and pray every day
hoping that He would never
take you away,
but He still didn't spare my heart
and bless you to stay.

So yes, my heart was torn
and faith was worn
because I felt all my concerns
went unheard.

Then when I feel I've got nothing left,
I still hear people say, "You are the best."

Kendra "Niki" Benford

So I lift my hand to you one more time
like I'm making a wish in the wishing well
with my last dime.

My mom never believed in failure
and gave me tons of motivation.

It just feels like I failed
and lost that great sensation
because the world that's cruel
left my heart completely spacious.

You never gave up on me
so it's really unfair if I do that to You
even if I really don't mean to.

Whatever's meant to happen will happen.

I just have to trust my One True Captain.

Kendra "Niki" Benford

Zodiac Heaven

When a Scorpio fell in love with a Cancer,
they thought they were making an
intimate disaster.

Instead they made their best
happily ever after.

She made a mighty fine Leo
that sometimes let her mind
override her mouth
when she saw things her way
like Ms. Cleo.

When the Scorpio decided to flow
with the wind,
the Leo sadly lost her soul within.
The Scorpio was sassy and strong.

The Leo was supposed to be
the same way,
but lately,
she has been doing everything wrong

Kendra "Niki" Benford

all because she wanted
her Scorpio to stay.

The Leo has been begging her angels
to guide her way
and has been getting knowledge
from her Cancer.

But it's not making the pain go away
any faster.

She tells her Cancer she is good
to move on,
but she keeps hearing her Scorpio's song.
This is what makes the Leo's heart
to scorn.

The Leo loves a Taurus;
they are best friends
just shed in different skin,
but the eyes feel like the Taurus
is the devil within
ready to drown the Leo in sin.

She screams out for the Scorpio to help,
but it cannot respond...

Kendra "Niki" Benford

What will the Leo do
if she falls before dawn?

As time grows
and the Leo takes what life throws,
it remembers the faith
and the Scorpio's love whispering,
"It's ok to get things wrong
as long as you continue to be strong."

It was the Scorpio's time to leave,
but as to the gift of that Leo it said to thee,
"You still have much to receive."

The Leo had one thing left to say.
"I love you Scorpio,
and I'm still not sure what to do,
but I know I will always miss you…"

Kendra "Niki" Benford

Face Your Fears

Poem from my mind exited from my heart
sometimes desiring a new start.

Love is hard to keep
because sex has become easier to find,
but with all relationships or friendships,
it comes down to being based on time.

Stay strong in the love
of the company you keep.

Never put lust ahead
to get a quick nut in the next person's bed.

The best love held is
to hold on near and dear to yourself,
and keep the rest on a shelf.

Trying something new,
"Yeah, I'm down for the cause,
but I'm just not ready for the damages
that will happen when I fall."

Kendra "Niki" Benford

If men just like women
would take care of home,
it will then leave room
for the significant other to stand tall,
and the other won't have to worry
about losing them at all.

Getting too involved or invested
into someone that knows
they're not ready,
that just leaves you in harm
and a little unsteady.

Exploring each other
even though it sounds tempting
and exciting,
I just don't want to make myself
too inviting.

My heart speaks volumes
while my body wants touch in value.

I'd be lying if I said I didn't want it
or wonder just as much as you,
but my heart normally tells me
what to do.

Kendra "Niki" Benford

If someone's heart is not in it,
why even try?

Experiencing it if you can't have
the full expectation,
I want true dedication
and to be someone's motivation.

Many times, I wondered
about friends with benefits too,
and that however, it's true,
but I also have a sound mind
and heart too.

Venerable to a tee, but all I have left is me.
My daddy raised a queen
not someone's one night or booty call,
if I can't be treated like that,
then I don't need it at all.

Getting to know you is cool
but that's all I'm trying to give to you.

If something changes along the way,
then it shows you were meant to stay.

Kendra "Niki" Benford

Changed behavior shows
a person character.

I like the new her that looks back at me
because that means I passed the test.

I still smile with the best.

Grown as to what I know I need,
I just need help
finding someone to take the lead.

Mommy's no longer here
so she can't hug me or wipe my tears.

She left and whispered, "Face your fears."

Kendra "Niki" Benford

Kendra "Niki" Benford

Mommy's no longer here

*so she can't hug me or wipe
my tears.*

She left and whispered,

"Face your fears."

Kendra "Niki" Benford

Conclusion

I never really understood my purpose in life. Trusting God was always a constant struggle.

I fought hard to get to where I am. Now I can see what my purpose is and what my God was pushing me to.

My God wants me to fight for my life and inspire others to do the same, no matter how hard the struggle may seem.

Strong family support and The Good Lord above is how I have been able to overcome.

About the Author

Twenty-nine-year-old Kendra "Niki" Benford was born and raised in Fayetteville, North Carolina.

Diagnosed with cerebral palsy when she was an infant, Kendra never allowed her wheelchair to define who she was or what she was capable of becoming.

"Growing up with a disability wasn't always a walk in the park. I suffered with many insecurities then, and I still have some insecurities to this day."

However, the author is proud of the fact that she was able to overcome a lot and became a better person in the process.

Every heartache she encountered may have knocked her down, but they never kept her down. Kendra has a bubbly personality and wears her heart on her sleeve.

Her goal is to help people and to inspire them to do better.

"Sometimes I believe I try too hard and take on the problems of the world. I have to realize they are not my problems to take."

A pure-hearted, compassionate, and talkative person, Kendra is also known for her candor and tries to "tell it like it is if people ask for my opinion."

"Sometimes my mouth gets me into trouble, but that's just the type of personality I have."

Kendra's parents raised her to know that anything worth having, is worth the fight and she fights for her purpose in life.

Kendra loves children. She graduated from Fayetteville Technical Community College with an Early Childhood Education degree. Her desire is to be a teacher's assistant.

Butterfly Typeface Publishing

Contact us for all your

publishing & writing needs!

Iris M Williams
PO Box 56193
Little Rock AR 72215

501-823-0574

Made in the USA
Columbia, SC
24 November 2017